Bread

Claire Llewellyn

SEA-TO-SEA

Mankato Collingwood London

This edition first published in 2005 by
Sea-to-Sea Publications
1980 Lookout Drive
North Mankato
Minnesota 56003

ISBN 1-932889-38-8

Printed in China

Library of Congress Control Number: 2004103743

2 4 6 8 9 7 5 3

Published by arrangement with the Watts Publishing Group Ltd, London

Series advisor: Gill Matthews, nonfiction literacy specialist and Inset trainer
Editor: Caryn Jenner
Series design: Peter Scoulding
Designer: James Marks
Photography: Ray Moller unless otherwise credited
Acknowledgements: Nigel Cattlin/Holt Studios: 12-13. James Davis Travel Photography: 11c.
Mark Edwards/Still Pictures: 11tr. John Hulme/Eye Ubiquitous: 1, 18-19. Mostyn/Eye Ubiquitous: 15b.
Brian Pickering/Eye Ubiquitous: 10. Judyth Platt/Ecoscene: 11cr.
Thanks to our models: Edward Evans, Reanne Birch, Khailam Palmer Mutlu, Jakob Hawker, Casey Liu

Contents

Our daily bread

Most of us eat bread every day.

▶ *We eat bread at breakfast...*

4

at lunch...

Think about your day. When do you eat bread?

and at dinner, too.

5

A good food

Eating bread is good for us.

▶ *Bread helps us to grow and stay healthy.*

6

Bread gives us energy. Pasta, potatoes, and rice give us energy, too.

◀ *Bread gives us energy to run around.*

Many kinds of bread

Bread is eaten all over the world. There are many different kinds of bread.

How many of these breads have you tried? Which ones do you like best?

Bread is made from wheat

Most of the bread we eat is made from wheat flour.

▶ *Wheat is grown on farms.*

As wheat ripens, it turns from green to gold.

Farmers cut the ripe wheat.

Making flour

The part of the wheat that we eat is called the grain. The grain is made into flour.

▶ *Grain from the wheat is crushed into flour at the flour mill.*

Flour can be white or brown, to make white or brown bread.

13

Making bread

To make bread, flour is mixed with sugar, salt, yeast, and warm water.

Warm water

Flour

▶ *They are mixed together to make bread dough.*

Sugar

Salt

Yeast

Bread dough is soft and stretchy.

Sometimes the dough is rolled and patted by hand. This is called kneading.

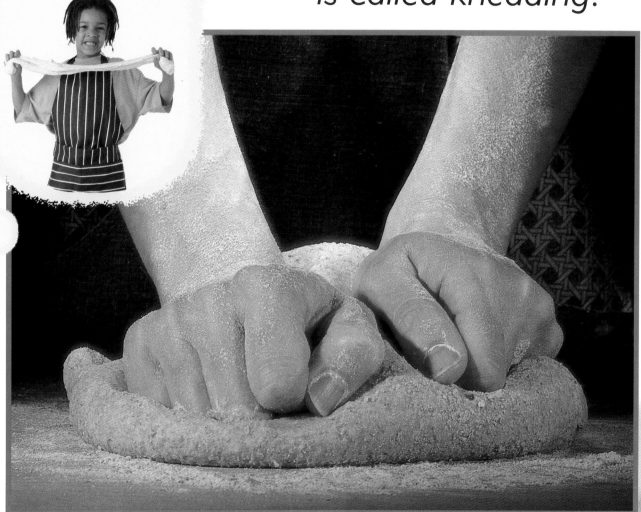

The bread rises

The bread dough is put into pans.
Then the yeast makes it rise.

▶ At first,
the bread dough
is flat like this.

To see how yeast makes bread dough rise, stir 1 teaspoon sugar and 2 teaspoons dried yeast into 1 cup of warm water. Soon the mixture begins to bubble. These bubbles form inside bread dough to make it rise.

After about two hours, the bread dough looks like this. Now it is ready to bake.

Baking bread

Most bread is made at big bakeries. It is baked in very hot ovens.

▶ *Bread turns golden as it cooks.*

Once it is cool, the bread is sliced and put into bags.

Where do you buy your bread? Do you buy it sliced?

19

Pizza!

Bread dough is also used to make other foods, such as pizza.

Put the dough in the pan, then put pizza toppings on the dough.

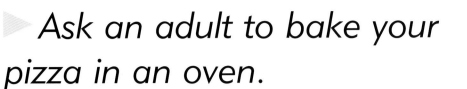 *Ask an adult to bake your pizza in an oven.*

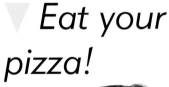 *Eat your pizza!*

Can you think of other foods that are made with bread?

I know that...

1 Most of us eat bread every day.

2 Bread helps us to grow and stay healthy.

3 Many kinds of bread are eaten all over the world.

4 Most bread is made from wheat.

5 Wheat is grown on farms.

6 The wheat grain is crushed to make flour.

7 Flour, salt, water, sugar, and yeast are mixed into a dough to make bread.

8 Yeast makes bread dough rise.

9 Most bread is baked in a hot oven.

10 Bread dough is used to make pizza.

Index

About this book

I Know That! is designed to introduce children to the process of gathering information and using reference books, one of the key skills needed to begin more formal learning at school. For this reason, each book's structure reflects the information books children will use later in their learning career—with key information in the main text and additional facts and ideas in the captions. The panels give an opportunity for further activities, ideas, or discussions. The contents page and index are helpful reference guides.

The language is carefully chosen to be accessible to children just beginning to read. Illustrations support the text but also give information in their own right; active consideration and discussion of images is another key referencing skill. The main aim of the series is to build confidence—showing children how much they already know and giving them the ability to gather new information for themselves. With this in mind, the *I know that...* section at the end of the book is a simple way for children to revisit what they already know as well as what they have learned from reading the book.